SO-EIA-262

SPINNING JENNY

11

NUMBER ELEVEN

BLACK DRESS PRESS

11
SPINNING JENNY

Number

Published by Black Dress Press
Post Office Box 1067
New York, New York 10014
Please visit us on the web
at www.spinning-jenny.com

Copyright © 2010

All rights reserved. No part of this work may be
reproduced or transmitted in any form or by any means
without permission in writing from the Publisher.

Spinning Jenny™
Black Dress Press™

Spinning Jenny welcomes the opportunity
to review submissions.
Please visit our website for guidelines
and subscription information.

Editor: C.E. Harrison
Art Director: Adam B. Bohannon

ISSN: 1082–1406
ISBN-10: 1-887672-06-0
ISBN-13: 978-1-887672-09-2

Spinning Jenny is a member of
the Council of Literary Magazines and Presses.

This book meets the guidelines for permanence and durability of the Committee on
Production Guidelines for Book Longevity of the Council on Library Resources.

This publication has been made possible, in part,
by a grants program of the New York State Council on the Arts, a state arts agency,
and the Council of Literary Magazines and Presses.
Spinning Jenny is extremely grateful for this generous support.

Printed in the United States of America.

ABRAHAM SMİTH
ELAİNE BLEAKNEY

EMİLY FREY
MİCHAEL MORSE

SAMUEL AMADON
RİCARDO MALDONADO

MARA VAHRATİAN
FRED SCHMALZ
STEVE BARBARO
BRİDGETTE BATES
THOMAS COOK & TYLER FLYNN DORBOLT
MEGAN LEVAD
JOSHUA BUTTS

JARED HAYLEY
ELİZABETH WİNDER

JOHN HARPER
ANDREW ABBOTT

LİNDSAY BELL
CAROLİNE KLOCKSİEM
MATTHEW PENNOCK
TOMAZ SALAMUN & JOSHUA BECKMAN

ANDREW SAGE
CHARLES FREELAND
ANGELA HUME
DAN ROSENBERG

ERİC ABBOTT
CLAY MATTHEWS
JENNİFER MACKENZİE
DEBORAH FLANAGAN
WİLLİAM WİNFİELD WRİGHT

ABRAHAM SMİTH
ELAİNE BLEAKNEY

EMİLY FREY
MİCHAEL MORSE

SAMUEL AMADON
RİCARDO MALDONADO

MARA VAHRATİAN
FRED SCHMALZ
STEVE BARBARO
BRİDGETTE BATES
THOMAS COOK & TYLER FLYNN DORBOLT
MEGAN LEVAD
JOSHUA BUTTS

JARED HAYLEY
ELİZABETH WİNDER

JOHN HARPER
ANDREW ABBOTT

LİNDSAY BELL
CAROLİNE KLOCKSİEM
MATTHEW PENNOCK
TOMAZ SALAMUN & JOSHUA BECKMAN

ANDREW SAGE
CHARLES FREELAND
ANGELA HUME
DAN ROSENBERG

ERİC ABBOTT
CLAY MATTHEWS
JENNİFER MACKENZİE
DEBORAH FLANAGAN
WİLLİAM WİNFİELD WRİGHT

SPINNING JENNY

11

NUMBER ELEVEN

!+Nº*

Abraham Smith

fred rose and hank williams in a writer's room
and ain't nobody ever
has known what
went on behind
that leaden handle door
the great wide door
that whipping walloper
this is already a great fat lie
for the door was a papery thing
it was one of those
after the war doors
the south after the war doors
it was a door that apologized
for itself when you shut it
still harbored a certain
hurtin' insecure sweet tea
cuts your toe off dye a beet cheese
shake rage light memorize
like maybe remember bone mumble
every slam or soft shoe shiv handle
and one day when
the whole shebang falls in
will tell it true to the earth
the book of the bunch of

prune eatin' cretins in cake hat heads i'll tell you
the floor under the door the grand
sweep if you will
marry me stump
of sundays
door was an ash tree
a thirsty thirty soldier mouth
with a low cave for the dead
was an ash tree
visited by squirrels a nit and
several hundred jays
jays are oil drilling equipment
they give you the sense
of the haughty rich with
a rubberized tip and a wing
like sky got a knife
for each millisecond's
birth and death and bridal shave
here honey where
the tree leaves have done
their dying this is a fine
bone pard
you don't have to shoot
a leopard in argentina
sit down supine
snow angel leaf
erikson with a whale
bone brush sir if it is
not too intimate look i am not
asking you to drink rain

from the creases in my cupped hand
but you who remind me of my
brother's son you with the sparrow's
cribbed nonchalant exposures
common you can
roll down all your windows
and no clothes your whole
body who would care?
whip your poor
it was mustard greens
between the teeth
that spiced the whole
rat pack of lies yes good old
hank sang 'em like he was going
around denting
half paid off cars
suspendered fool
with his underarm sweat
dark on this white the man
wore two snakes and had
a dark patchy underarm sweat
like a dying soldier's cave
full of bones how to happy
happy is as happy does
so i nabbed a cave bone and i
hit the dust and up flew the cave
and i was hired fourth
in the race for ineffectual
platitudes the plat map
went extinct the mats

under the dying dead looked
intact but when you touched them
they went to allergic
mist i seen five jays holding
their noses and the son's
father saying no sir i won't
take the radiation and the fierce
flat delta cropduster's turning
another whining thunder and
the morning wine totaling
three holies and five unholies
and every little sparrow as
a negative number equals
the sky must have spit them
all you honky tonking angels
know that kidneys ain't the rage
in heaven nor
dicks and that's why
in the land of the pure
you can throw your dick down
jay jay jay you can throw your
poison hauler your purifiers
your kidneys your livers your
kinder your timber kippers
down all down hawk and
owl pacifier and prowl
prow and canon through the
rectum no rectum silly this is
heaven on a slow train all
there is is wings and bending

things as you touch them go
to wind or mist this is
looming large this this
teetering won't quite spill ten pin
every writing is a long coy bone
fuck you without the fuck
bulges at the edges where it connects
every song bone poem was
once a sung sun reading
how and where to howl
or hum along by the light
by the light by the light of the
last cave bear's long tooth every one
took them for goners but ever wonder
why the good yogurt is only
available on the coasts?
suicidal instinctual rippling coasts
where the ground shaking
one day offs you
and yours and eels
long as the senile's list
of chores she keeps writing
save milk from the dark
cold for the night is
a dandy with a cop's dream
of tearing thunder can't touch
a teacher's need to please
my childe roland williams
my rose like a blood
never forgotten the soil

remembers all
says what was
almost on a lark
soil is spanish for who cares
random murmured by the
prettiest woman in the history
class full of shy
crass blurs might be the last
and first word are you tired
yet? just stand there a little and let me
bowl you down you dizzy ten
here's a buffalo on ice skates and here's every
territory you ever spoke me
into the wheel ditz over
iced up bison steel flash
topple hurry gird chief i am saying
hank was a dirt and it's hard to
find a dirt a sparrow's
old joke of a poor man's fork
foot hasn't kicked come ye
worm to the dance
of my wings i am saying rose
was here you have a window
and what do you want to look out on you can
build your earth out of potato shavings i would not
lie to you gardenias are an awful
shame they are just a joke green
they are garden with a try at
doing some flipping fun to the ear
you might as well go around

singing i saw the light with
a half turned to stone mastodon
leg bone is that a bonnet at the top?
o rose o rose for all your
we move via internal immovability
the heart of the deal is still the leather pouch
full of pulled teeth the cave man
wears around his neck as
memory of conquest
and song you can take a tooth
from the dead or you
can go around dancing
just try it for one minute
jigging to every bird song
you hear it will plum wear you out
i made my move when the bear
smiled
fish at the back of the throat
all guppy pouting blues
i snatched up the locket
full of quiet teeth they weren't
teeth they weren't that violent
they were seeds
in shapes of fears
they were pain like a spine
could be a rope and one end
some sumo angel
did his thing in river flood sand
and then there was below
a devil in a french hat

smoke smoke smoke
and you never knew when
they would twist and you couldn't
trust them to switch out
the raveling rope and you wouldn't
want to referee the thing
there are lines to cross
how many times in this life
have you heard the words
it was only a game
red bird on his shuffled red card passing actually
batted that rose concussed it
for the next thirteen seconds
thinks it's lincoln in a hat top
daddy long legs with the wound
dresser i saw god
bending low before him in a bow not a word
not a word in passing yes
with every word inside him
also bowing bending
plant their heads to double grow
plant their leaves to spell the bees
coyote
tongue out
clearly winded clearly
by the mailbox
wash my seeing
with two aprons
on fire for body legs
legs what you called her

and legs what a wind
run out the house
winded with the flaming thing
and you beat it on the earth
smoke and dirt
smoking dirt
many sooner sidle lethe ward
she was your daughter's
favorite rug she gave
the rug a girl's name
she said alice lord
those salad days
winding charm
easter is not just for christians
anymore easter is for
lovers tennessee is for cicadas
through cement for love
the lord made trees for love seats for birds for almost
nothing flying sings
unless it's get away get away hoi hoi
like there was just plum run out of gas animals
all over in his blood
and deserts and tents where
rattle gourd musics and smoke
and tongues turned into
parrot's dicks had long all
fallen into char war ululating
it was like his whole charmed walking structure
was a hieroglyph for drinking
and the only thing really ridiculously hard

to fathom was why
o why are bottles so small
if you are born for one
you'll never get over
the mountains of glass
you mow through
more the scarecrow
he died in texas
'bout 900 miles south of moline
doubled over and his face went black
overdubbed good night irene
out of oxygen
because his lungs and his heart
got into a little close
stock tank drowning
and they say he died in texas with a water
moccasin snail poop boot but the
thing is they saw it and got him
out the car and let him walk around
hank hank hank hank can you
hear me he was always a blues singer
and when he died he almost became who he was
in a way he never was with mama he was
forever low on the back seat
or mama cake knifed or billie jean sparrow lord her velvet head
looks down looks left
and lofts a lined descent
seedy offering touch this
no don't rough it easy
with it in your hand

cement was once
sand our human
chemical louisiana
put a book ban on tribal heals
the question you've got to keep
asking is why in the autopsy was he
beat up bad why has no one
ever talked about that
was it the moon
potato gunning canned
beers at old hank? no one told the poor
it is easter look at that car mooing
either a drunk left it on or she vacuums
the rooms this easter morn
sound of a plane
we are all so used to
going to do a fly over at the game
flying is about killing
just like everything is
mechanics wise about
hurrying death to
them who'd wish it hurried here
but does anyone really wish it? okay the
hot heads in cages
chewing cars the hawks
with the code in their guts
to unlock the mountain
but does anyone really
love country? should the
country lovers have to

prove it? should they have
to hump trees and suck
rocks and occasionally
be seen with a bag of birdseed
dumped on their person
and just these really intelligent
jays jab jab god
wretch a cornucopia
all the cardinals
playing bingo
chisel on your neck
and you with a butterknife
missing the slit on the screw's head
so cutting little gouges in the wood
and there are things for whom
this gouge on the jamb be gorge and any
neighbor wants to wonder you
are just getting an open heart
chipper from a cardinal you
are just then misgiving a valley
to a spider when surely some day who knows?

Send

Elaine Bleakney

I text him from the carousel: "the horses are free."
I text him from my horse glassed under the Manhattan
    Bridge.
I text him from someone getting married to the left to the
    right.
I text him from my horse nostalgic in the mouth.
I text him from the same heart to the lights; my phone can't
    spell "hurdy-gurdy."
My horse is from Idora, Ohio. She splinters

to whisper, whorled in it, *he is not the point*
—the public one I keep meeting:
a smaller island
made of this, tugged around the Hudson to
tug around the Hudson boulders the glacier scraped
out of us. Our shallow-bedded trees.

Being

Elaine Bleakney

professional not wanting friends. A city
a few people I want to walk
under a Ricky's

umbrella. These umbrellas with you, cheapos
blooming them up. A city
some people I want

off as they

umbrella. Mottsu Sushi guy crocked in his
"Mottsu Sushi." Walking out
of him. Daily. Down

in my cup. The situation with you
in the wall: no hole between our cubicles. My horse
a souvenir Oaxacan turtle
waving her brain

installed.

Stay on the Sharp Side of It

Emily Kendal Frey

Dear Jalapeno,
Dear Carcass,
Dear Sunset—
There are seeds
in the teeth of this.
There's a net covering
the tarmac.
Dear Tether,
Dear Sweetness,
Dear Hull—
Run quietly to
the robin's nest.
Seal the tomb
like a shoelace. A question
mark burns its dot
on your lower back.
Dear Artichoke,
Dear Floodlight—
Ratchet up what you
can of midnight.
Pinch it twice.

Void and Compensation (The Good Connolly Brothers)

Michael Morse

According to the Sunburst annals,
the Connolly's have up and moved to Dublin—
a maze incalculable to the drinking mind
but a hearty new home nonetheless.
Think of it, the elderberry brother says,
our secret lies not in praise but in travel.

I'm not so sure, what with all the chrysalis girls
in transition while I, lay-low butterfly, rest.
I'll dangle all summer for a change and
wait the Gal Fridays out of the woodwork,
but not the good Connolly brothers:
would that grace and fear make Churchills of us all.

They'll tap the wires and collate spellbound
birds who obsess the post-rain groundswell.
(Penniless deprivations I'd just assume forget.)
I love those guys; I'll wish them well and wait
for my sun and her solstice interventions
of speech—for every blemish there's a Stet.

Void and Compensation (Last Quarter)

Michael Morse

No overtime. Because we see our rose,
and when the curl comes, as to hair, its head,
weak neck, inevitably droops as if its lids
can remain no longer in light, need sleep,
because little packets offer small sustenance
and the water powdered has taken on
a sheen and some silt, because the scent
that fills the house now takes the hallway out,
because we'll snap said stalk in two, throw
out the thornier version and, stuck,
bleed a little, see some crimson, and think
a colored runner to a gilt chair might make,
if we would walk it, our footing, our odds,
and our over; because we play to win,
because we will not tie but go for two,
all preparation garnered and playbooks dispensed,
and all wonderful things having blossomed
because what takes the hallway out must have
a plot out in the world, some trellis for its hat,
some ribbed safekeeping for the heartfelt,
we with the heavy heads—wake up—must sing,
because, because, because, because, because.

Void and Compensation (Second in Command)

Michael Morse

Take a secondary city, say, Reno,
which drags a bit behind Vegas, or Custer's Rosebud-
crossing Reno, Lakota whipped and glory broke, a xeno-
phile whose kingdom-come was Sioux and Cheyenne flood.

He's called a Queeg for having headed south
and leaving his General with troubles that converge
when reckless captains over-calculate their worth.
They'd rather have lamenting tabloids sing a dirge

on their behalf, so here's a little snack for you, scout:
don't let arrogance drive you up on bridge or bluff;
take a little time to sum up and make out
which routes pass for fortitude and those too tough

given the geometries we plot from positions
on high—fame's runners-up sometimes are sages
provided they meet what they've met with contrition,
if only to cut and cash the future's forgetful wages.

Landscapelessness

Samuel Amadon

Imagine apple orchards without trees
was not a dream. How do you make make do?
Some conversations lead to more like few.
Like thoughtful absence, yes. Then fingers keys.
Like turning eavesdrop into speech with please
excuse, at times I find the self see-through.
Here one who captions every picture who?
Here one who asks are there no more degrees
on this? Then hurls the oven through the wall.
Whatever you've been building, brother, needs
to break itself itself. Imagine legs,
now using them how saunter rhymes with brawl.
Why here's the dancer who has led, who leads?
A commonality was begged. Like begs.

Logarithm for Tinderbox

Ricardo Maldonado

Much of wood, much of river—
I hoped I were a bird, among other
objects of your regard,

to set myself upon the work
of hymning:

hapless about hills, out of a furnace,
out of a sea of coal, largely

excerpted. We look at one another,
post-communion and profusely

dentured. I am to remember my living,
how ended I could be,

hiding my crest somewhere along
the ice yard.

It feels unfinished, expect for the Midwestern
clouds.

Being ungraceful at slaughter,

I learned from some other monochrome wind
report, now obsolete on the North side.

The radio program patterns umlauts as rain.

As for the Mark

Ricardo Maldonado

About a two-day trod, I proposed,
chipped canary objects:

root cutters, hurtled
and unstoppable. I make no bones about,
not today.

Chewing ropes,
I labor my shoulders sewn.

Welcome to clutters,
little Orion.

On Translation

Ricardo Maldonado

The newspaper report proves milk
to be useful for current. One could assume it.
The effort conducts to the reception
or the cell, where I, taxidermist, other leper,
am prompt and startled.
A spokesman hosts a funeral
to answer questions about tubes.
My hypothesis: the confessors met the cross,
which led to electricity.
One moves where biographers
formulate a complex amongst the grocery.
Copulate when one is of rope
age, and agree to bladeless travel.
The performance is elementary
or worse: I have visions of pigeons.
And he, the philistine,
is proud of the fluorescent appendage.
There, the crest and small pox fellow,
and the radio, part conductor,
part crude.
Somewhat destitute, the face survives
the turbines of winter.

FROM *Soaptrees*

Mara Vahratian

That's feet on the pedals or a tin can drag, skip-skip.
Shortfingers researched contradictions: to wear pearls, not.
    Bouquet
a won't be, think my smile (little dope) gauzy
and kudzu down the back. The stomp at the restaurant after.
Call it received.
Feathered headwaters, look at this place   dirt to the
    hilt,
your second-best bed just leaned-to, block
the heat out, block the door, soaptrees.
Another lost summer tossed her head—you come back

to the Cavalcade of Homes, preferred a fall-out
shelter and bunkered against fastening (to what)

look the walkway or sweep it, hoard
all you slept through, put-up hair, memorized
rubbing. Was just my side wasn't a damn thing.

*

Dinner plates. We request your presence underground for to carry up tulip bulbs. It necessary, came printed on fine onion-skin and told so. I run out my winter hours against the mountain-line, torture you with those big eyes. When living in a dollhouse back away from his stepping, laundry. Think a book of etiquette and scuffed boots, Shortfingers hop off your bike   don't mind. Forty miles from Dee-troit this is nowhere. A whole series of going to's and landed on her smart, boy-cut panties—what bother the town or any old way of I have done well or not, tried to wind out the twine or drink you under. Failed miserable, biographies all night long and now can safely say my man, go leave it to that other lost Catholic in his big bad glasses. In sung. What I am good at: kale, short answer, history. Will run after your bike, regret it. Sister has also at a man's feet, done hit the floor then cast him off, wore inside him 'til he didn't know better from let. *Although   you treat me   badly.* I madly. Darling won't you go and grown your hair, bang-bang. I thought kit, the post on June sixteenth, backyard arsonist tactics. Slept through movies to remember 'em better. What's your hearing these days, does it span or collapse in the canyon. You say how do you remember. O, it's just behind me and tempting look. Green awning rhymes with you-guessed-it. The fit and color are nice, some modern detail but in the dishwater—slip. Smile, I kind myself.

*

Doctor's will and orders by which I mean come to me please and you are a look at small houses, geranium baskets, seafarer beard grown at Barnegat, ye cockles and feet clamming up the bed. From bobbin to bobbings a love story stares out its good eye, for—I have ate what you gave me (Father K: *how so*) and canned too many peppers for the row. Once upon a sweet har-monica we sounded out names and said quickly what we didn't want; that bowl full of Clovis points, eight seasons nigh on. That's a yard-measure, come what July not of this place we thought on it and pulled down eyelids the Murphy beds. Coined a massage to know drifters, tipped mail-slot open to itself a collective ah-ha, collection. Stamping out a seal of approval I keep a good house, am handy and handled. With sandalwood soap I'd fain have something, an odor or other, wringed and strung upside until you pioneered on through.

Practical applications

Fred Schmalz

I am trying
to say trashcan
I am trying to say
small paper bag

there is a large spill
where I was and I am
holding a broken-lidded cup
apologizing I am
sweating thinking how

will I distract the baker
his helper makes
matters more harried
Why don't you
go home why don't you
give me that

If only
and then please
try to understand
I am raining
all over myself

Landscape (with Sanitation Worker)

Steve Barbaro

but the point right before Graffito says *tar-*

based trash gar-

bage—the garbage: it is!   gar-bage!

that point before Graffito
is saying *sick bags!   sick!*

—yes at that point before Graffito is just talking he is eating.
he is eating cuttlefish

and cheese

and Dutch bread. he is chewing and speaking, such as *the
garbage.* such as *the trash.*

and the dishwasher is running and
Blake said some stuff

about "a rural pen."

and Graffito is eating and reading Blake and imagin-
ing Blake awash in rapids

also carrying a house that shack

the widower's shack Graffito used to see
downhill from that house

the house Graffito grew up in.

Flood Watch

Bridgette Bates

First the lightening, then the car alarm
lighting up the alley. We were tired

beyond eventuality; we dug
into an aluminum blanket.

Forgiveness became a mutual decision.
Mutually, we walked to the station

in the morning, our pants cuffed
away from the flooded sidewalks.

A woman volleying an umbrella
at her fingertips, it twisted into

a small claw. We were tired
and decided it best to let her fix

her own beside the stands of three
newspapers, three rivers pictured

under different verbs. The river -blanked-
as we directed ourselves in different

directions, forgave the standstill
in the silver turnstile.

Through the arcade of vending machines,
past a man confused by button placement,

through Charleston, through her
sitting across from us on the train.

On a scale of one to ten,
do you think we will make it?

FROM *Monster: a Glottochronology*

Thomas Cook and Tyler Flynn Dorbolt

Lend me please your ability (top shelf) to interpret the stayed words & images into a pattern that lets me circumnavigate by important guises of the (turtle) city. This is a double-decker (snapping) flip. The whip has a feast of (beastly) possible points of connection. If I needed you to really guess that I was baptized in harmony with the concretes, I would simply (wave) ask you to initiate a live trap somewhere along the 57 line. Your baby has boss knees. (stampede) Erect heels. Outfit them. The smashing vandal has (alleyway) peach pits for the storyteller who goes away in the summer. Pardon the landscape, I've given myself over to more elegant (shaved) prose. If I am wafer-thin & wanting a reach-around how can I order it upright? (!) Nevermind how I wallow in the walking these (swallow) shoes can do, I've got my eyes on the last grape-squeezing hussy & she gallops like a fucking rose petal in the heat of the blue desert apart from it all (whoof). Canned jewels (concentrate). I make a sardine an entire fishery (turf) I pluck a bad mint from my pocket & whirl it in the effervescence like a merry-go-round (go) hunting hobgoblin with two ears to wind & a nose o'er the fence, Charlie. I am also (surf) quite small. I tuck a sock in a drawer & dream of living rooms with matching (crevices) furniture where I am fulfilled by thriftiness & the dinner I have prepared on $3.67 without a hitch (hour) in the globe for the foreseeable. So pin it, sure &

the queasiest of jurrs smoothes out to a ch sh ch near the clothes basket nearly. (fa-ra-ra) What of the breakfasts? (burr) Undulate a crown in a pea-pod & wake up wheaty. (fanatical) I hold a phone in the buffalo carcass & wait for an answer. I pitch a cord of wood (checkered) I romanticize the skillet-flip. (bird) Because that's where it (lines) will be. Almost a festive kick in the prairie. The rib-ring (fortification) resounds in wagon (roulade) or wheeled & good-wooded (steamer) I see the long distance of our insistence on festering the real road. Once (creeping) because twice out-looked (hands) I did nothing but Quinoa our famished lilt. Any more time (keepsake) with you soldier & the tannins (beading) will become too (airy) noticeable. The last beholder of ova only wanted you sweetened white until the shadows of the 30s made sense of suspense. She (spank) we have given a guise (enclosure) to dinnertime (plates) partied (rolled) out our decay for moping patterns & juices for the (quaint) strangulate. Somewhere along (jumping) also wants of web. This is the grim skin (favor) a veal terrine with fava bean f r e c k l e s as olive-oiled (limpid) as the extra virgin of Cappezzana: carrying rivers (iota) of rumination wayward: a meeting (guest) place on sinus scourge. Of see-sockets (next) seas pocketed vis-à-vis being— they go inward & reef (cannibalize) treasures until depth is measured approachable (candle) they go below oar-roaring labor (popover) tending toil.

She has a shone bone (gear) as heirloomed as our chanting leer. Our discourse (steaming) is a distasteful (candelabra) pasta course. Our silence uses Ragu. Scraping the speech (trusty) I truffle her lingerie. I actualize or (but) coagulate in the (quiet) viscera of vivification that allows the trooping of your sleep (automatic) to storm me Gulliver. (dancing) Great to know the dam dipped & farmers kept (honey) out the pre-swirl, proved a (pitch) squeal is (raw) pebble talk in acre-craze. Milk into the percentage because I want the dairy off your teet dear (knotted) Spring. You will petal, you will silken the straight clock & chime into shorts. Now I drag my foot. The harp (little) busted, so I need a new (baby) axiom. I wail. (cramp) The entire flotilla made a break for it when they saw the ranges (brimming) coming at them with out-of-tune & dirty forks vibrating above their heads (bustle) to the rhythm of the falling bodies of sick livestock (picnic). We call these artfully arranged granite slabs the yard. Notice the saplings that (stock) will be given the duration of this present (elder) company to (yeast) make their mark in the historical bark (chance). Even the enclosures have been (bore) drawn & quartered to fit the hampered (chute) intellects. I made a stir in the pudding & out came the (muscles) shape of the stir. When the calls come I dodge a fat grappling whimper (dash) to tell me what is happening & I gorge myself (sate) on the plentitude or unremitting machine (pound) sounds. Why have I come to this factory? (simple) In the sick hope of upbringing myself with the grapevines of pre-wines? With the hope of extracting (decanting) the syrup from a clearing? (transport) Let me undo the briskness (back) here & shimmy down the jojoba & make a (physique) cosmetic. Here, we value both angularity (slit) & (wound) roundness, we have a place for each (reach) & they allow that we sit (Indian) & feel comforted.

(open early) Hurry me the pass, I need a superfood. Now more than ever (teeming) I hear cavorting is out of fashion, so instead I (& honey) call this guaranteed fuck of my singular a nation (scalp) finding its economy. I refilled (raw-sugared) my bottle of water.

Guilt, On the centrifugal force of

Megan Levad

Why don't you just spin me
harder, swing me right
out over

the roof,
deep
into the snow-
filled pond.

I'll bob there

come melt,

a walnut, soft and green,
rind-ready. I'll stain

everything you touch
when you fish me out.

Shyville Road

Joshua Butts

Woods cede to farmland
and the State University extends

operations to include aquaculture
(and among so many farms).

e-mail is oyster something
and letters addressed Dear State Fair Dog Agility Participant

find their way through the mail to the
mint highway signs that announce

a silver spinning budding aquaculture—
spawning pools, tadpoles, cruel young life

a rifle's bullet from American Centrifuge.
American Centrifuge? Mint sign.

Take a right at Wakefield Mound, then a left
at Nursing Home, or just take Shyville.

You can huddle spawning pools right up to it?
Well, man makes the biggest machines

for the biggest causes that of course
call for the biggest solutions.

Could there be a county-sized, steam-filled iron
and some wealth of fabric

to stitch and press the perfect poor person's uniform
for hiring day? Any need filled.

What was this wiped-out town called?
Shyville.

My wife's forebears had a habit of naming communities
after themselves.

Here's a print.
Lester Shy on his horse, Custer, captured by

a Brownie No. 2.
Photography 1910, not hot to trot, but stationary boy!

The swish of the tail is fuzzy, the only imperfection.
Spoiled by our slicing shutter speed,

no more hallucinatory ground up cigars.
A pile could smoke you a mile to some

bandied about bridge where to cross
you take a stand on local politics.

But what if you don't know the area?
Assess, quickly, or guess.

Let the 18-wheelers ride with the Amish.
Then mutter Shyville, Martin Marietta, A-Plant, aquaculture

with trace quantities of transuranics
like descendants who collect custom glass.

Custom glass sometimes pulls folks apart,
two brothers waiting for a relative to die.

There are trees and surely one cloud
and a few people who remember Shyville.

Yes. There was Lester's sister.
Her true Penelope was Beaver Creek.

Red Hollow Road

Joshua Butts

Cars parked forever
under the crab apple.

Why'd they all show?
There's a stage

in the back-hoed
shooting range,

the scalloped land
and the dreadnoughts

strung to the peculiar
note of the afternoon.

Some have fires.
Some have brittle fingers.

A man has a horse called Banjo.
Bring a covered dish.

Hello, Goodtime.
Welcome out.

*

With lights like light for the biggest
coon hunt,

Jim White's Pinto chases
a fox to the end of the bridge—

but these are foxes
that sally near trash cans,

no arctic foxes
on Red Hollow

except for trips to Beaver
for a euphemism.

The wild out here
are to be trusted.

Far out here
isn't that far out.

*

The grass is sprinkled
with flowers of blue, purple, yellow and pink.

The deputy for beauty in the county
will be rewarded

and though he tries too hard
may his yawning reward

warmth in the morning,
coolness in the afternoon.

His jeep—bright orange
blasting Foreigner

from forest to water—
kernels, seems ready to sprout.

*

I've brought the most insulting side dish.

*

Deer season done,
Christmastime,

rural yards become cities,
roads turn safe.

Throughout the night.
tears adjust themselves.

The lights get turned on.
The tailor needs an extra button.

The actors disassemble.
The commandments are simple.

*

When the pauses between arrows
reach twelve minutes

eloquent young men from the town
play a stretch of country music.

Then more arrows, and after three callers
trim the turkey boxes—

the cancellations begin.
Too many roads, too much wallpaper to hang.

The car bivouac, the preferred concert
and the bellies ache all night.

*

Remember me when I become a soda.

*

In the morning the war is over.
We cram our homes into cars

and follow the customary gestures of daylight.
One highway sign seems to read:

Come lovers to the cone zone,
we've got a chill

and so many children show up
the cinema offers free matinees

and the silver vat baked beans are traps
of wiles and wiles and wiles.

Help me with the humming conscience
I'm scared to go on.

FROM *Vanishing Point*

Jared Hayley

3

The steady rain did more
than fall, and often
the diversity of living things
seemed like a drawer full
of old keys. Vapors
labored, liquids squished,
rug burn marked rebirths.
We loved so much so hard,
that when the blur took form
in our vacation photos,
the clock's continuity
and the cruelty of the creator
seemed weathered into the bricks,
identical strata dispiriting
us independently and in total.
The easiest way to look busy
was to be busy, but we were
beside ourselves. No obligations,
no applications, no intimations.
Surprise and satisfaction
came in waves
but never concurrently.

Waters went slack
at least twice a day.
Rain evaporated
before it reached the earth.
Only instruments
could detect a life.

7

The counterfeit currency
had proven too difficult
to part with,
so another, emptier,
relentlessness
took us up.
We with little
but symmetry
to go on.
Once
we had abandoned
the project wholeheartedly,
our proposals were leaked
back to us
in the margins
of an indictment
of the Platonic solids.
Most of these
methods were inaccurate,
others were accurate
but opaque.
Those we adopted
moved from
to do list to to do list
unchanged, impossibly overdue.
We hid these
on the ends
of typewriter ribbons,

on the inner grooves
of our difficult psychedelic LPs,
under the grubby rubber
of the floorboard mats,
in the box of obsolete rechargers,
across the length of the watch
fob and chain.
Check stubs
covered
weeks' frames.

8

Day circled night
until they wore
the same outfits.
They gobbed up our globe,
promising at least a hint
of becoming eclipsed
by the obvious. Well,
we were everything
he was and of which
she was made,
which, while narcotically
distracting, generally sucked.
It was a seduction
to follow his sighs,
but an impropriety to witness
her sobs. We bathed
in our weakest attitudes;
spent galaxies clustered
in soap scum and humdrum.
The brightening
we thought revealed
the original heart
was stolen, no doubt,
from our own
campfire show.
Those who played
us were flame
crystal wearing folk.

None lived well.
We paled
with the very thought
of ourselves.
The game was strange.
Wind caught paper,
paper caught wind,
but soon became
themselves again.

Dr Julian's Aversion Therapy Was Not Working

Elizabeth Winder

Trim Twin,

my nights are Spoil Islands.

               (Set the flag)

         not kin

         nor given.

Now Trips a Lady, Now Struts a Lord

Elizabeth Winder

Lost my cat-

gland in the Chat

    Sanctus

    (sans-culotte)

    blot

from view, My Wick

    You—

Grafted a Scale of Herring, Herring

Elizabeth Winder

Lappets and tails—

(the pointe of her *ne*)

Dead

fun from the middens

down.

Seldom Gold

John Harper

Still alive to be broken softly
to the ground of my since-fled pictures—

I see how little of an expert I am—

And how hard it is
to pretend to be ok—

What can I declare—seldom, seldom
I take an action, clear in me,
through my undulating, congressional layers—

That symbol coming down the road in such
and such a speed—I don't know what that means;

and that symbol coming down the road
in such and such a manner, I don't know what that means.

And I am on that road, too, as a standing symbol,
and I quake as such a such.

I guess I am on my head on my hands,
my burnt, burnt hands
aching for warmth—

NINJA BROKEN HEART IN ME
Andrew Abbott

COUCH ON THE EDGE OF ETERNiTY
Andrew Abbott

TIBETAN HAM
Andrew Abbott

APOYA DONDE
Andrew Abbott

VOODOO
Andrew Abbott

TREE ROOT RIVER
Andrew Abbott

WRITERS BLOCK
Andrew Abbott

NIGHTMARE ABOUT A PIANO

Andrew Abbott

That Big Old House Has Roaches

Lindsay Bell

She expedited her ventures by staying put
as a single particle may interfere with itself.

All the doctors threw their hands up,
unaccustomed to this quantum illogic.

The seasons then belonged to her, cinnamon
and gravy, drags from cigarettes a guest left,

she, pinching the snubbed butts like bugs.
Forefinger, thumb, carapace, she was chaste

as the wind and whatever was blown with it.
The insides went first, veins once knit

lost their opacity. Soon, visitors could see
through her, like a fine sheet of mica glass.

For several instants a day, she became two places
at once. But really, it was just a geometric trick.

Transanimal

Caroline Klocksiem

I do so go
after ghosts . . . it's easy enough.

Someone comes back
as an Apaloosa,
his nostrils flared like paper.

Someone comes back from far away, driven,
blackened, by an angry cabbie. One day

someone put a cold key
in my kitchen and I put it
in my hand. It happens

every day. Wednesday there was
someone with a yellow cat. She was
a very tired devil cat. She went to sleep
with her eyes dark and opened. Then she

came back as brass, as
my key. I go. I let her go.

Beneath the Arctic Floe

Matthew Pennock

This shrewd quotient,
spiraling and ridged like the fractal
geometry of a seahorse tail.

My new obsessions: electoral math,
Greenland sharks,
the doctrine of duck and cover.

Portrait of a symptom on the couch:

Sleeper, we are blind
and sometimes
eat our own.

The bed, too empty.

Sleeper, do not fear.
If you are buried with mortar and brick,
you have become too heavy.

Buildings do not collapse
due to fire or some
architect's mistake.

They grow tired simply—
our asking them to hold us.

Walsenburg

Tomaž Šalamun

translated from the Slovenian by Ana Jelinkar and Joshua Beckman

All these cities are the sun, Walsenburg.
The sun, the sun. With Maruska and Ana
we go to the post office, full of flags.

In bars it smells like in Colorado.
Ants rushing over the floor, laborers
moving steel springs, tracks cutting across roads.

The take-off is a long-distance call.
Oh, what a thin animal the domestic cat
is, beauty, which is the crushing

of joints, budding like vapor!
What a thin animal the domestic cat is!
What a city is Walsenburg!

Saint John of the Cross, Rubbed in Snow

Tomaž Šalamun

translated from the Slovenian by Joshua Beckman and the author

I don't know if I'm Poltava, as I'm stormed in vain.
Go on top of the black house and copy clouds.
Take a cat with you.

We were sunk in pots of milk when we came to the camp.
Here, before the way, a marten was shooting around,
after the war and inscription vomited into our eyes.

The Danube is not stocky.
The machine rattles, the table jolts, coffee storms.
I sob like a statue with beauty's defect abolished.

Curls are put over the hearth, I walk on the white
embers. The girl that will lose what is put around her
shoulders, didn't yet sink into my consciousness.

Slaves, they're really prisoners, evaporated.
They remind me of my mother's flesh.
David's hand is too big.

Barbara Richter will give me an apartment on
Uhlandstrasse. Diran told me yesterday
I was a Stalin-like zealot wanting

everyone to believe in God. Even
Terry sees it. Nuns jumped from the heights
on his bones. My curls are cut.

One Thousand and One Nights

Tomaž Šalamun

translated from the Slovenian by Joshua Beckman and the author

It smokes from the fridge.
The sun. The sky. The wine.
Pine needles on red earth,
across the bay, the oak.

Deep is the body in the sea,
in the golden mandorla.
The sail splashes the face,
a dunked salty deer.

We're swimming to the other island.
Straight, straight rocks.
The heather is violet, green brown,
the soil is eager.

Rhetoric of War

Andrew Sage

A rowboat is ineloquent on land,
How fortunate, then, that there is water, a lake of it
Floating idle or jerked along

By inept oars. The beautiful wants me separate
But I can't defend
Over-green water, homeless sun, the goose flotillas
(Cameras around their necks).

Why does the beautiful want me to fight wars for it
When the sun is this hot, the geese so benighted,
The water so honorably still?

Ergo Mother Goose

Charles Freeland

Illness radiates outward from the impact zone like rumors. Or those salesmen who have a quota to meet and can't agree on which strategy is best. That perfected by the nuns in their hovels. Or that first sketched out on construction paper by juveniles trying to imagine a world where they are no longer situated at the bottom of the ladder. Where they are appreciated for the pleasant aromas that emanate from their mouths. It's like they always say—watch the bugs with brightly-colored legs. They got that way for a reason. But maybe the gift of olfactory sensation, when it's taken to such heights as one finds in the wolfhound, can filter through the hazards that hide from the mind otherwise, like pennywhistles. Or the bone fragments that float about in your hand for months and even years after you've scraped it across the concrete in a fall. Or been escorted out the way I was—meaning by two or three women so beautiful and ultimately wrongheaded, I couldn't help but consider them refugees from some draconian set-up in the warehouse district. Victims of their own alluring present. And the void that had settled in behind their breastbones like a cousin come from the Midwest, dragging his suitcases behind—his manuscript copies of the Polonaises and Mazurkas he had been working on all summer.

FROM *Second Story of Your Body*

Angela Hume

As if I'd been touched but—

                                             (his head
                                             pouring out).

For now, a best-case
scenario:

(some)story wastes
into myth—

(terrible as it is,
it is)

a half-life, a calculable

horror, though eventual,
a blister of light.

Reeking and bold as only
the wealthy

(if it had been

yours, we say, imagine

the waste).

From the train
the bay, a blister, or bluing

steel. History, whelm
the myth.

How Do We Avoid Living in Jersey?

Dan Rosenberg

I meant to say
something else entirely to you

listen, I have no gauges, what is Jersey
but island of holes filling

Sometimes I forget to breathe then lightheaded
there you are

in the Hudson River
fishermen drop sparkling threads

you slip in your earrings
& my mouth opens to your neck

to get not around but through Jersey
bite down on a pomegranate seed

I Am

Dan Rosenberg

I am the final tissue, the one
most steeped in divinity.

Sometimes I am one of those cups,
the only ones allowed in the heart.

I am painted brightly to catch the eye
which remains because of my sleep breath,
my utility. I am the most.

I am the accordion note.
I am like you times seven
and way better with ladies.

I have a mane and ribbons and
roaming inside me. I know how to use.

I'm often used in a crowd.
I am that part of the rug,
the empty center of the apple.

With the rabbis closing in, riding my wake
over the united, over the Earth and
my hips, my door, my islands

and fog press the air.
My sloth, my tree
my tree sloth
filling my voice.

"The Longest Time" (mixtape, circa 1993)

For Molly and Mark

Eric Abbott

Of the mostly unmourned lost arts, the mixtape will be most missed by lovers, those late-night sculptors, tuneless musicians trafficking in the near at hand. Sadly, it's all "stream my playlist" now. Doesn't the world know that love is always scrawled in Sharpie, a penslip away from gibberish and inconsequence? Doesn't the world know the best things take the longest time? If a mixtape is born of desire, born of a will to make love more than a list of tired songbook standbys, it is born again every time the late-night clock tolls on some sentimental hipster stationed before a device designed to garble intention, consigning his love to chance-cancelled confession. If the mixtape, if so . . . only poetry could be more inept. If you want to communicate, use the telephone. If you want more, a mixtape's gonna hafta do. How will modern lovers know what's true, when nothing is difficult, when some she knows some he's hand has never hovered hesitantly over those clunky buttons half the night, hoping she says 'no' to sleep and 'yes' to him? Makers of love, compilers of mixes, what's the difference really? A narrow stairway of proper, tumbled down. If not difficult, how will he know if she is the kind to hand-rewind a history whispered into existence, recently come undone, and not the kind to string it all out the window, to be found by some sad man collecting cans in the roadside abyss. After all this, after all this time, after all. No, a mixtape requires more. Now, flip the tape, begin again at wonder, the blank side of today, another mystery of instances: more windy beaches, new restaurants yet, death, of course, and love—a new life, curled in the curvature of belonging, some-day, as to a lover, all secrets meanings revealed. How we go on: the cover song whose disparate renditions we covet.

Market

Clay Matthews

The produce store but the tomatoes still
aren't good. I say produce beauty. They lock
up at night behind chicken wire. And will
the city sleep? Darkness about the block
and I get a special kind of sat-is-
fac-tion watching teenagers wipe out on
their bikes, watching the streetlights shake and fizz
on and off again. The graveyard upon
the hill reads to all of us at night, names
father, names mother, names the dearly be-
lovèd. From my seat I look at the frames
on the wall, I look at the dog and see
in his eyes we are thinking the same thing:
red tomatoes, ripe, the gone things dreams bring.

Stiffener Compass

Jennifer MacKenzie

Stiffen and then bend
double: it is how they
think you. A whistle
emboldened by anger

a fissure in a bouquet of
overcoats pushed through
Fallen forward in the white
noon slept like the dead. 3pm

woke with a wreath of smoke
smiling in my head like cormorants
trailing leashes: she is addicted to
the fathers and likes to take them

out not really cooled. 3:15
wind wrapping its long feathers
around the island and you become
your father looking at the ground

Or leave her an egg. A face
drawn on it in wavery thin pen

a sad egg smile. Sometimes
a melon. I drew off my shirt

in the dark swiftly, sweating
An archer dreaming in the lobby
Of all the fantasies, which
is the one that prevents her

I Spend Three Nights in a Whale's Belly

Deborah Flanagan

scared in the way you decide you'd rather die
than move or breathe. If I sit very still I can retain
my human shape. She seems to have room for me.

This place, smeared deep
in the whale's belly, fills with words
that leave my mouth and lose their courage.

Whales decide when to breathe I discover; she can't fall
into an unconscious state for too long before sloughing
off the next breath as she slowly spirals and lolls.

There are reasons for resisting
language—one of them is love. I press
my lips together.

It's difficult to shape the air precisely as I attempt
a teeny scrap of sound. Parched and keening,
I practice weeping at different pitches and velocities.

In a song of four notes,
unhappiness fills her four-chambered heart
she uses my wail—

On the third day the whale dies. She falls
down through the ocean slowly over the course
of a long day; all the fish watch her:

Gentle descent, despite her heft,
she displaces the water—
my stomach flips as we sink.

32 Fucking Poems about Chess

William Winfield Wright

1.
Make your move
make your move
make your move
make your move
make your fucking move
already.

2.
It wasn't until
I played sober
that I realized how
fucking boring
this game is.

3.
I never call it fucking
but wouldn't it
be better than this?

4.

Where's the fucking checkers set
and don't tell me
we'll have to use these guys.

5.

Two rooks chase each other
around and around and around
while the kings just sit.
Fuck.

6.

You lifted your finger.
No, I didn't.
You lifted your fucking finger.
No, I didn't.

7.

I hid three of the pawns
one queen and that weird
fucking horse thing.
Try playing now, asshole.

8.

I get up for coffee
I get up to pee,
and if I catch you
moving the pieces again
I'll fucking kill you.

9.
I'd like the bathroom
or maybe a kitchen
in this kinda pattern.
What do you think?
Just fucking play!

10.
My dad taught me
how to play baseball
hit grounders at me
until I chipped a tooth,
the stupid fuck.

11.
When those intellectual
shits stayed past closing
to play out some game,
we'd throw the ashtrays at them,
those big fucking metal ones.

12.
I had that dream again
where I'm a pawn off the board
and the queen's already been taken
and we are talking and she's laughing
and then the game is suddenly over
and she has to go back
to her stupid fucking husband.

13.
This is really great
waiting for your letter
opening it, reading your move,
making a move of my own,
writing back to you.
It's a good thing we'll see each other
at the fucking Star Trek convention, huh?

14.
My bishop just fucking ate
your queen's lunch, pal,
and there's nothing you can do about it.

15.
concentrate now
concentrate
concentrate concentrate concentrate
concentrate
oh fuck!

16.
Actually those trophies
aren't for playing chess,
baby.

17.
You're not gonna get up
to play on the computer, are you?
I want a fucking divorce.

18.
Wait, I thought the Sicilian Defense
was where some guy named Vito
cuts your fucking head off.

19.
You can't do that.
You can't do that.
You can't fucking do that.
Oh, ok.

20.
What's all this fucking crap
in the mailbox?
And why does it have
my name on it?

21.
OK, I'll play
but if you are going to comment
on every fucking move
with that fake British accent,
I'll quit. I swear.

22.
Nah, I don't want to play
with those guys in the park.
They smell fucking awful,
and they always kick my ass.

23.
Yeah, I love that movie,
but it's not Death he's playing with
but this fucking weird guy
with a black robe and a scythe.

24.
Look over there, table twelve,
the way that guy rubs
his temple, and her
right there biting her lip,
that's fucking sexy.

25.
Pick up the house.
Pick up the fucking house.
Stop sitting on your fat ass
complaining that the match
was rigged and
pick up the fucking house.

26.
Yeah, I know
it's part of a pageant and all
and you get to walk around on a chessboard,
but are you really going to wear that?
You look like a fucking idiot.

27.
What do you mean
you're not going to serve me?
Do you know how many points
I'm away from being a Grand Master,
you stupid fucks?

28.
She did everything wrong,
tried to move the pawns backwards,
kept touching my pieces,
resigned every game with,
"How about a movie?"
and I'd tear my fucking arm off
to see her again.

29.
Really, bishop to g7,
and then he did rook to h7,
and you did, what,
queen to g1 check?
I don't give a fuck.

30.
Then I saw it all laid out,
the whole thing, like a dance,
twenty moves to mate,
and I started laughing.
And I was laughing and laughing,
hysterical, tears coming out of my eyes.

And the bastard resigns,
calls me a fuckball
right there and walks out.

34.
That fucker,
ten years old at best,
and she smashed me,
pinned my queen,
got up two pawns,
and checkmated in 13 moves,
smiling all the while
through those big fat braces.

32.
This moves that way
and this goes diagonally
and if you get here you can trade.
Now let's try it together.

NOTE ON THE TYPE

This one's for Chowderhead.